Weather

Martin Skelton and David Playfoot

Contents

All in a day

A sunny morning

It's morning. You pull back the
curtains, and look outside. The
sky is blue and the Sun is shining.
You put on your shorts and
T-shirt, and run to school.

A wet afternoon

By the afternoon, it's wet and breezy. You're feeling cold. Thank goodness, Dad's brought your sweater.

Weather changes

The weather can change from one moment to the next. A sunny morning may cloud over. A wet and windy morning may be followed by a dry afternoon.

3

Weather patterns

In some parts of the world the weather doesn't change every day. It's more settled.

Hot and dry
In North Africa the Sun feels hot all year round, and there is little rain.

Hot and wet
In parts of South America the weather is always hot and wet.

4

Icy cold

The North and South Poles are so cold that the land is always covered with snow and ice.

Each country has its own kind of weather – like a regular pattern. We call this the country's climate.

The seasons

In some parts of the world the weather changes regularly during the year in a pattern which we call the seasons.

Rainy and dry

Some of the warmest parts of the world have two seasons – one rainy, one dry. It all depends which way the winds are blowing.

The four seasons

Cooler parts of the world have four different seasons – spring, summer, autumn and winter. One season slowly changes into another as the Earth moves round the Sun. Plants and animals sense the changing seasons, and it affects the way they grow and live.

What causes the weather?

High up in the sky, things are
happening that we cannot see
or feel.

Great winds blow backwards and
forwards around the Earth. They
rush above wet seas and hot
deserts far below.

The Sun shines brightly, warming the land.
Huge parcels of air rise up into the sky.
They cool, and sink back down towards the land.

All of these things help to make the Earth's
weather. Sunshine, wind, clouds, rain, snow
and thunderstorms – all of these things
are happening somewhere
in the world right
now.

9

The Sun

All our weather begins
with the Sun.

The Sun in space

The Sun is an enormous
ball of super-hot gas. Its
heat reaches us through
millions and millions of
kilometres of space.

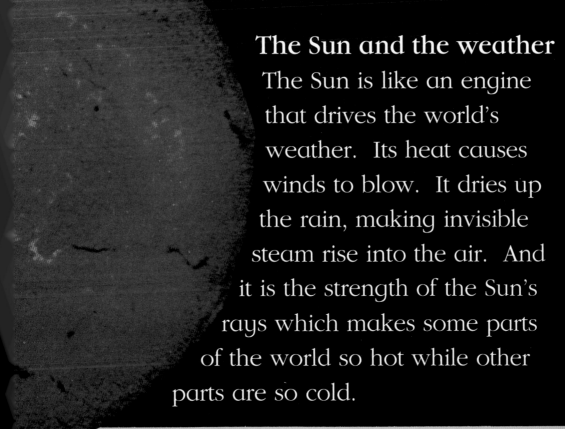

The Sun and the weather

The Sun is like an engine that drives the world's weather. Its heat causes winds to blow. It dries up the rain, making invisible steam rise into the air. And it is the strength of the Sun's rays which makes some parts of the world so hot while other parts are so cold.

Clouds

What are clouds made of?

Clouds are made of tiny drops of water and ice crystals, floating in the air.

The water comes from seas, rivers and lakes. It comes from the rain, and the puddles you've splashed in. The Sun's heat changes the water into invisible steam. The steam rises up, changes back into tiny droplets of water, and makes a cloud.

Cloud shapes

There are different types of clouds. You see high, wispy clouds on a sunny day. But heavy grey clouds often bring rain.

Rain

Rain may be wet, but it's very important. Without it, we'd have nothing to drink.

It's raining!

Rain falls when water droplets inside clouds join together and become too heavy to float. As they fall to the ground, they keep on joining up with other droplets, getting bigger and bigger all the time. By the time they hit you, they're wet!

Rain around the world

Rain does not fall evenly around the world. Hot deserts have very little rain, because the Sun's heat is too strong here for clouds to form.

Snow

Like rain, snow comes from the water droplets and ice crystals inside a cloud.

Inside a cloud

When it's very cold, the water droplets inside a cloud freeze onto the ice crystals. This makes the crystals bigger and heavier. They begin to join together, making flakes of snow. Big snowflakes are too heavy to float, and they fall from the cloud.

Will it snow?

If the air is freezing cold all the way down to the ground, then we have snow. If it's not, the falling snowflakes melt, and we have rain.

16

Wind

Wind is moving air

You can't see the wind, but you can feel it on your face, and see how it makes the trees sway. Sometimes the air moves slowly as a gentle breeze. But sometimes it moves fast as a strong wind. Strong winds are powerful. They can damage houses and uproot trees.

North, south, east, west

A wind is often called after the direction it is blowing from. A wind blowing from the north is called a north wind. Wind can bring hot or cold air from other places.

19

Hurricanes

Hurricanes are terrible storms with very strong winds. They are sometimes called cyclones or typhoons, and they usually start over warm, tropical seas.

How do they begin?

Hurricanes begin when rising air starts to spin above the sea. The wind spins faster and faster in a shape rather like an ice-cream cone. On the outside of the cone, the winds blow at over 300 kilometres an hour, but in the middle of the cone, the air is perfectly still.

Danger!
Hurricane winds
can flatten buildings
and fling cars across
the road.

21

The food we eat

Think of all the plants we eat – rice, wheat, fruit, vegetables and so on. Without the rain and sun, they simply wouldn't grow.

Plants in different climates

Different plants have different needs. Without the right weather, some plants wither and die. Orange trees need a lot of hot sunshine. Rice plants need rain. They like to stand in water.

Water for life

We depend on the weather for our food. If there is too little rain, plants don't grow. This is one reason why many people in the world are hungry.

The clothes we wear

How do you choose which clothes to wear in the morning?

Hot or cold?

People who live in countries with very settled weather wear similar clothes every day.   In the warmest parts of the world, people wear loose, light clothing to keep them cool. In cold places, people need to keep warm. They wear thicker clothes made of wool or fur.

A bit of everything

In some places the weather changes from season to season, and sometimes even from day to day! Here, people need different kinds of clothes to suit the weather.

25

Getting to work

Weather can make it difficult for people
to get to work.

Deep snow
When heavy snow blocks roads and railways,
it's impossible for many people to travel.
They are stranded at home until snow
ploughs clear the roads.

Strong winds

Fishermen get used to wet and windy weather out at sea. But when the wind is very strong and the sea is rough, they leave their boats in the harbour and stay on shore.

Hot sun

Hot, sticky weather makes you sleepy. No one feels like working then.

How do you feel about the weather?

The weather can affect the way you feel.

Hot, but not too hot

Most people enjoy warm sunny weather.
But if it's too hot and sticky, you start to feel
cross and uncomfortable.

Wet, but not too wet

A soft spring shower is sweet and refreshing.
But no one likes it when it rains for days.

Feeling stormy

Some people love a
thunderstorm. They enjoy
the flashes of lightning
and the deafening
thunderclaps. But many
people are terrified by
the noise, and can't
wait for it to end!

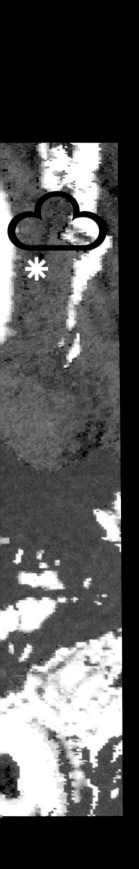

Weather forecasting

When people need to know what the weather is going to be like, they make sure they hear a forecast.

Balloons and satellites

Scientists who forecast the weather use many special instruments. Weather balloons fly high up in the sky, gathering information about the air. Further out in space, weather satellites send back pictures of cloud patterns. They also follow the movement of winds around the Earth. Every day, scientists use this information to make the forecasts you hear on the radio and television.

Index

HarperCollins Children's Books

A Division of HarperCollins Publishers Ltd, 77–85 Fulham Palace Road, Hammersmith, London W6 8JB

First published 1994 in the United Kingdom

Copyright © HarperCollins*Publishers* 1994

Prepared by *specialist publishing services* 090 857 307

ISBN 0 00 196544 1

A CIP record is available from the British Library

Illustrated by Maggie Brand

Photographs by B & C Alexander/Still Pictures: p5; David Austen/TSW: p23; Jo Browne/Mick Smee/TSW: p24; Bryn Campbell/TSW: p5; Mark Edwards/Still Pictures: pp24/25; David R Frazier/TSW: p26; John Garrett/TSW: p12; Cheryl Graham/TSW: 13; Joseph Green/Life File: p4; Graham Harris/TSW: p22; Arnulf Husmo/TSW: p27; Life File: p8; NASA/Life File: pp10/11; TSW: pp4/5, 9, 10, 11, 16, 17, 25, 29; SYGMA: p21; Darrell Wong/TSW: p18; Lawrence Livermore Nat. Lab./Science Photo Library: p30

Series editor: Nick Hutchins; Editing: Claire Llewellyn; Design: Eric Drewery/Susi Martin; Picture research: Lorraine Sennett

Printed and bound in Hong Kong